Dear Parent:
Your child's love of reading starts here!

Every child learns to read in a different way and at his or her own speed. You can help your young reader improve and become more confident by encouraging his or her own interests and abilities. You can also guide your child's spiritual development by reading stories with biblical values and Bible stories, like I Can Read! books published by Zonderkidz. From books your child reads with you to the first books he or she reads alone, there are I Can Read! books for every stage of reading:

SHARED READING
Basic language, word repetition, and whimsical illustrations, ideal for sharing with your emergent reader.

BEGINNING READING
Short sentences, familiar words, and simple concepts for children eager to read on their own.

READING WITH HELP
Engaging stories, longer sentences, and language play for developing readers.

READING ALONE
Complex plots, challenging vocabulary, and high-interest topics for the independent reader.

ADVANCED READING
Short paragraphs, chapters, and exciting themes for the perfect bridge to chapter books.

I Can Read! books have introduced children to the joy of reading since 1957. Featuring award-winning authors and illustrators and a fabulous cast of beloved characters, I Can Read! books set the standard for beginning readers.

A lifetime of discovery begins with the magical words "I Can Read!"

Visit www.icanread.com for information on enriching your child's reading experience.
Visit www.zonderkidz.com for more Zonderkidz I Can Read! titles.

HOORAY!

_____

can read this book!

"Sovereign LORD, you have begun to show to your servant your greatness and your strong hand. For what god is there in heaven or on earth who can do the deeds and mighty works you do?"

–*Deuteronomy 3:24*

ZONDERKIDZ

The Beginner's Bible Heroes of the Bible Collection
Copyright © 2011 by Zondervan. All Beginner's Bible copyrights and trademarks (including art, text, characters, etc.) are owned and licensed by Zondervan of Grand Rapids, Michigan.

Requests for information should be addressed to:
Zonderkidz, Grand Rapids, Michigan 49530

ISBN 978-0-310-72827-6

The Beginner's Bible Noah and the Ark ISBN 9780310714583 (2007)
The Beginner's Bible Moses and the King ISBN 9780310718000 (2009)
The Beginner's Bible Queen Esther Helps God's People ISBN 9780310718154 (2008)
The Beginner's Bible David and the Giant ISBN 9780310715504 (2008)
The Beginner's Bible Daniel and the Lions ISBN 9780310715511 (2008)

Illustrator: Kelly Pulley
Editor: Mary Hassinger
Cover and interior design: Cindy Davis

Printed in China

12 13 14 15 16 /DSC/ 10 9 8 7 6 5 4

ZONDERkidz

I Can Read!

SHARED READING

My First

The Beginner's Bible

Heroes of the Bible

Noah and the Ark

pictures by Kelly Pulley

(Noah) waited seven more days and again sent out the
dove from the ark. When the dove returned to him in the
evening, there in its beak was a freshly plucked olive leaf!
Then Noah knew that the water had receded from the earth.

–Genesis 8:10–11

A long time ago, people
were very mean to each other.
They forgot about God.

They did not love God.

This made God very sad.

But Noah was a good man.
Noah and his family
loved God.

God had a big plan.

He told Noah,

"I am going to start over."

God told Noah to build a boat.

The boat was called an ark.

And Noah did what God said.

God said, "I will save you.
I will save your family
and two of each animal."

Noah built the boat.

God sent the animals.

"Hi, cats and dogs!
Hi, bears and birds!"

There was food.

There was family.

There were God's animals.

One day, God closed the door.
Then God sent a big storm!

Rain began to fall.

It rained and rained.

The ark rocked and rocked.

The ark bumped up and down, up and down.

Noah prayed.

Noah's family prayed.

The animals watched.

God took care of Noah.

God took care of his family.

God kept all of them safe.

The rain fell for days
and days
and days.

The earth was covered
with water!

"Shhhhh," Noah said.
Something was different.

It was quiet!

The rain had stopped!

The ark was still!

Noah said,
"Dove, please find land."
But Dove did not find land.

Noah said, "Dove, try again."
Dove did find land!

One day, the ark bumped into land. Slowly, the water started drying up.

God said, "Time to go!"

He helped Noah open the ark.

The animals went to play.

God said, "See the rainbow? It means I will not cover the earth with water again. I promise!"

I Can Read!

SHARED
My
First
READING

Moses and the King

pictures by Kelly Pulley and Paul Trice

" 'I will take you as my own people, and I will be your God.
Then you will know that I am the LORD your God, who
brought you out from under the yoke of the Egyptians.' "
—Exodus 6:7

God's people were slaves.

A mean king ruled the slaves.

Moses was scared
of the mean king.
So Moses ran away.

God wanted Moses
to help the slaves.
Moses did not know how.

One day, God spoke to Moses
from a burning bush.
"Moses, go back
and save my people.
Take them to a new land."

Moses was afraid.
"The king will not listen to me,"
said Moses.

"I will help you talk
to the king," God said.

Moses went to see the king.

"Let God's people go,"
Moses said to the king.

The king said,
"No! The slaves cannot go.
I do not know your God."

"My God is powerful.
You will see what my God
can do," said Moses.

God changed the river water.
Nobody could drink it.

The king said, "No!
The slaves cannot go."

God sent frogs.

God sent
bugs.

God sent
sickness.

50

Still the king said,
"No, no, no."

God made the sky dark.

Still the king said,

"No! The slaves cannot go."

"Let God's people go now!
If you don't, God will take
all firstborn sons," said Moses.

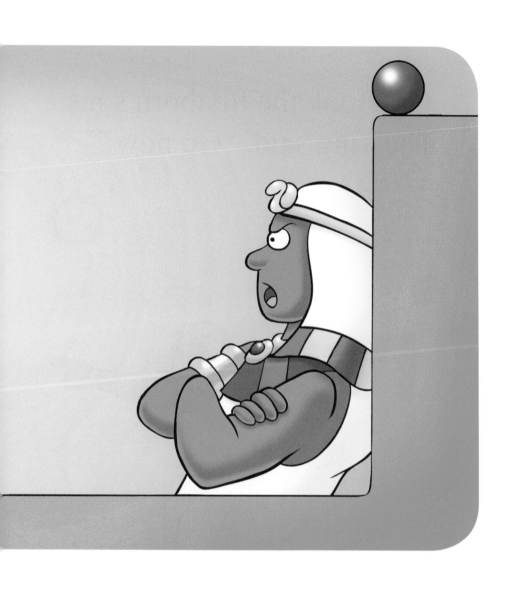

"No! The slaves cannot go,"
said the mean king.

God took the firstborn sons.
The king said, "Go now!"

So Moses led the people
out of the city.
They went to the Red Sea.

The king and his army chased
Moses and God's people.

"We are trapped by the sea!
What do we do now?"
the people asked.

God sent a big cloud.
The king and his army
could not see.

God said to Moses,
"Reach your hand over
the sea."

God parted the water.

Moses and the people ran

to the other side.

The king and his army
were close behind.

God made the water crash down
on the king's army.
Moses and the slaves were free!

I Can Read!

My First

SHARED READING

Queen Esther Helps God's People

pictures by Kelly Pulley

"For if you remain silent at this time, relief and deliverance
for the Jews will arise from another place, but you and your
father's family will perish. And who knows but that you
have come to your royal position for such a time as this?"

—*Esther 4:14*

Once there was a king
who needed a new queen.

"Let us find you
a new queen," said
the king's men.

Esther and Mordecai were cousins. They lived in the king's land.

They loved God.

KING'S PALACE

Mordecai said,

"You could be the new queen."

So Esther got ready.

And she went to see the king.

The king liked Esther.

He said, "Will you be my queen?"

Esther said, "Yes."

The king had a helper.

His name was Haman.

He was a mean man.

Esther and her cousin were Jewish.

Haman hated Jewish people.

He did not love God.

Haman had a plan.

He went to the king.

The king did not know
Queen Esther was Jewish.
The king was tricked!

God's people were in danger!
Mordecai heard about the plan.

Mordecai went to tell Esther.

"Esther! Save God's people.
Maybe that is why
God made you the queen!"

Esther needed a plan.

It would not be easy.

But Esther was brave.

She would help God's people.

Esther made a nice dinner.

She invited the king and Haman.

The king and Haman were happy. The king asked, "What can I do for you, Esther?"

"Haman tricked you!
You signed a law," Esther said.

"It says to get rid of all Jews.
I am Jewish!"

The king was mad!
He did not like to be tricked.

The king said, "Get Haman!
Arrest him now!"

The king made Mordecai
his new helper.

The king was happy with Mordecai.

The king was happy with Esther.

The Jewish people were saved!

Esther was a hero.

God used Esther to save
his people.

David and the Giant

pictures by Kelly Pulley

"All those gathered here will know that it is not by
sword or spear that the LORD saves; for the battle is the
LORD's, and he will give all of you into our hands."
—*1 Samuel 17:47*

Goliath was a big giant.

He was mean.

He wanted to fight
King Saul's army.

The army was afraid.

They ran from Goliath.

David took care of sheep.

He loved God.

David's brothers were in
the king's army.

One day, David took food
to his brothers.
He heard about the giant.

David said, "The giant does not scare me!"

"Let me fight the giant,"
David said to the king.
"God will help me."

"The giant is big,"
King Saul said.
"And you are too young."

"Please let me fight him,"
said David.

So the king gave David
armor to wear.

David said,

"I do not need armor."

He was not used to wearing it.

David picked up some stones.
He was getting ready to
fight the giant.

David saw the giant.

The giant saw David.

"You are too small.

I will beat you!" said Goliath.

"You will not beat me,"
said David.

"God will help me!"

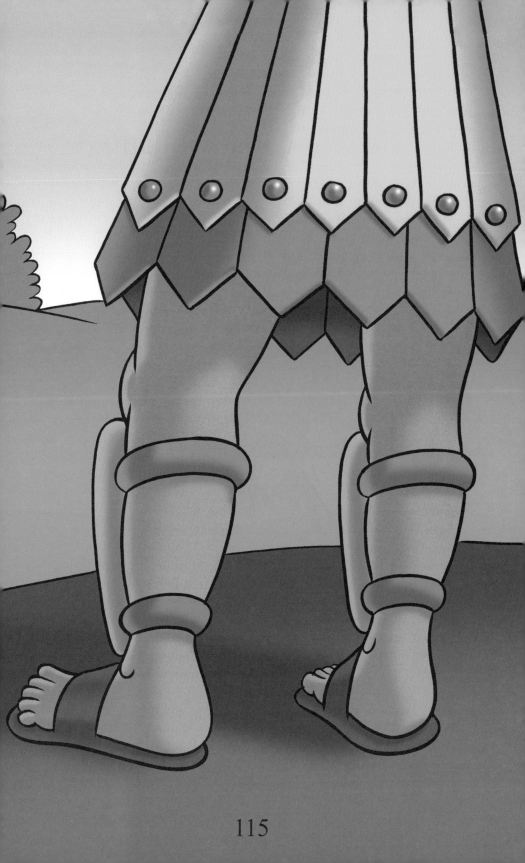

David took a stone.

He threw it at Goliath.

The stone hit Goliath
on the head.

Goliath fell down.

David won!

The men in Goliath's army
were scared.

They ran away.

The men in King Saul's army
were happy.

David was a hero.

"God is great!" yelled David.

"He helped me!"

The Beginner's Bible

Daniel and the Lions

pictures by Kelly Pulley

"My God sent his angel, and he shut the mouths of the lions.
They have not hurt me, because I was found innocent in his sight.
Nor have I ever done any wrong before you, Your Majesty."
—*Daniel 6:22*

Daniel was a good man.

He loved God very much.

Daniel went to the king.

The king loved Daniel.
Daniel helped the king.

Because he loved God, some
men did not like Daniel.
The men made an evil plan.

The men went to the king.
"King, you are a great man,"
they said.

"People should pray
only to you."

The men said, "If they do not,
we will put them
in the lions' den."

The men wanted to get Daniel
in big trouble.

The king said, "Okay."
He did not know it was a
trap for Daniel.

Daniel prayed only to God.

The men saw Daniel praying.

He did not stop praying to God.

The men told the king
about Daniel.

"King, your helper Daniel does not obey your rule," the men said.

"Daniel was praying
to God. Not to you."

The men had tricked the king.

Guards came to take
Daniel away to the
lions' den.

The king shook his head.
The rule said pray only to
the king.

But Daniel would not stop.

He would pray only to God.

The king did not
want to hurt Daniel.

The king said, "Daniel, I hope your God will save you."

Daniel was thrown into the lions' den.

The king was very sad.

Daniel prayed to God.
He asked God to watch
over him.

So God sent his angel
to help Daniel.
Daniel was safe all night.

In the morning,
the king woke up.
He ran to see Daniel.

The king called, "Daniel,
are you okay?
Did your God save you?"

"Yes," said Daniel.
"God's angel helped me
with the lions!"

The king was so happy!
"Come with me, Daniel."

The king told all his people,
"Daniel's God is great!
Let us pray only to God."

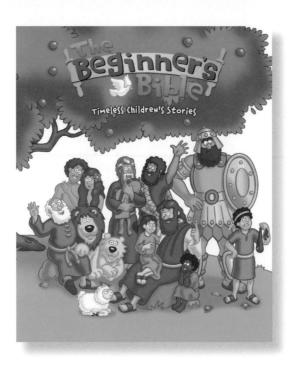

The Beginner's Bible
Timeless Children's Stories
Illustrator: Kelly Pulley

Introduce children to the stories and characters of the Bible with
this beloved and bestselling Bible storybook of all time! With
vibrant art and compelling text, more than ninety Bible stories
come to life. Kids ages six and under will enjoy the fun illustrations
of Noah helping the elephant onto the ark, Jonah praying inside
the fish, and more, as they discover The Beginner's Bible® just like
millions of children before. The Beginner's Bible® is the winner of
the Retailers Choice Award in Children's Nonfiction.
For online games, fun activities, and teaching resources, visit
www.TheBeginnersBible.com. And to hear what others are saying
and receive exclusive offers, become a fan of The Beginner's Bible
Facebook page!

Available in stores and online!

The Beginner's Bible Deluxe Edition
Timeless Children's Stories
Illustrator: Kelly Pulley

The bestselling Bible storybook of our time—with over six million sold—is now available in a deluxe edition that includes two audio CDs enhanced with compelling narration, music, and sound effects that help bring more than ninety Bible stories to life like never before. For online games, fun activities, and teaching resources, visit www.TheBeginnersBible.com. And to hear what others are saying and receive exclusive offers, become a fan of The Beginner's Bible Facebook page!

Available in stores and online!

The Beginner's Bible for Toddlers: Board Book Edition
Illustrator: Kelly Pulley

The Beginner's Bible® is the perfect starting point for
toddlers to learn about God's Word. With simple text,
bright art, and a padded cover, this cute board book edition
presents ten Bible stories in bite-sized chunks that kids can
understand. Help toddlers discover The Beginner's Bible®
just like millions of children before!
For online games, fun activities, and teaching resources,
visit www.TheBeginnersBible.com. And to hear what others
are saying and receive exclusive offers, become a fan of
The Beginner's Bible Facebook page!

Available in stores and online!

Series: I Can Read! / The Beginner's Bible

Beloved stories from The Beginner's Bible® are available in the I Can Read, My First level stories for young readers. Accompanied by vibrant art and compelling text from The Beginner's Bible®, these stories from the Bible are full of life and fun, and children can start reading about the adventures of their favorite Bible characters all by themselves!

Complete List of Titles:
*Adam and Eve in the Garden**
*Noah and the Ark**
*Jonah and the Big Fish**
Baby Moses and the Princess
Jesus Feeds the People
Baby Jesus Is Born
The Lost Son
Moses and the King
*Queen Esther Helps God's People**
*Jesus and His Friends**
*David and the Giant**
*Daniel and the Lions**
*Jesus Saves the World**
Joseph and His Brothers
*These titles are also available in Spanish/English bilingual versions!

For online games, fun activities, and teaching resources, visit www.TheBeginnersBible.com. And to hear what others are saying and receive exclusive offers, become a fan of The Beginner's Bible Facebook page!

Available in stores and online!